DESTINED TO DOMINATE

A HIGH SCHOOL SUCCESS GUIDE

DEMARQUIS R. BATTLE

DESTINED TO DOMINATE

A High School Success Guide

DeMarquis R. Battle

Printed in the United States of America

ISBN: 0692310177

ISBN-13: 978-0692310175

Learn more information at
www.battleleadershipgroup.com

BATTLE
LEADERSHIP GROUP LLC

BATTLE 4 CHRIST PUBLISHING, LLC

DEDICATION

I dedicate this book to my children. My hope is that you will dominate every obstacle before you. The words I pen will be relevant when you get the opportunity to read them. You are destined to dominate!

ACKNOWLEDGEMENTS

I want to give a special thanks to the students and teachers who gave their perspectives on the successes and failures of today's youth. The words you all shared were encouraging and will impact this generation immensely. I am grateful for your transparency and truly believe every student that reads this book will be better served by your testimonials.

TABLE OF CONTENTS

DESTINED — bound for a certain destination; ordained, appointed, or predetermined to be or do something.

DOMINATE — to rule over, govern, control; to tower above, overlook; to occupy a commanding or elevated position.

Get ready. You are destined for something great. You are destined to achieve new levels of success. You are destined to be set apart and to walk through new doors of opportunity. Get ready, because you are destined to dominate!

Get ready. You are about to dominate your high school journey. You are getting ready to walk into a greater level of dominance. You're getting ready to rule over your challenges. You are getting ready to control your daily approach to life. Get ready, because you are destined to dominate!

INTRODUCTION

Every person has a destiny. It is up to each individual to decide if they will dominate the challenges presented in life and ultimately walk in their destiny. The sole purpose of writing this book is to ignite a fire in tomorrow's leaders. This is my attempt to awaken the youth of this world and shake them to their core. This is my way of opening the eyes of teenagers who have been told that there is nothing for them to see; they've been told their dreams are unattainable. This is my way of activating ambition and pride into the next generation. There is a great purpose for your life but if you do not believe it, that purpose becomes invalid.

These next few years are critical for your success. How you spend this time can make or break you. I desire to see young men and women equipped with principles that can help them navigate through the murky waters of high school. I hope to instill some measure of wisdom so that students can make better decisions in their lives. I see future doctors, lawyers, musicians, government officials, and business owners in many of today's youth. But unless strong character is within them, they will never achieve that level of success.

Many students will be stuck wondering what could have been if they would have taken things more seriously. This is why it is essential to listen to the transformational tips I am going to share. I wasn't perfect in high school, but I gained valuable experiences that helped to shape my future. If you implement the principles I'm going to share, I believe you will be destined to dominate.

"The secret to getting ahead is getting started."

- Mark Twain

CHAPTER 1
IT STARTS IN THE 9TH GRADE

I can remember the summer before I started 9th grade. It was scheduled to be the best vacation time ever. For most kids, the summer symbolized freedom from the rigors of academic life. My family usually went to St. Louis to visit what seemed to be a million cousins, great aunts, and uncles for the annual family reunion. My mouth still waters thinking about the delicious barbeque ribs and carnival junk food that littered my summers. I remember the countless hours shooting hoops in the heat of the night. I can still hear the sound of my favorite jams blasting out of my radio. I can also visualize the water fights that went down in the streets. Our neighborhood dance parties at my boy's house were always off the chain! In today's terms, we would "turn up" for those events.

Everybody would meet up at the movies in the summer. I was so anxious to go hang out, that I didn't care if I had a ride back to my house or not. There were countless times my boys and I were left stranded and had to walk home, hoping my mother wasn't up when we got back. That was sure to be a death sentence!

During this particular summer in the middle of all the amazing events and lifelong memories, I was also preparing for the biggest moment of my early teenage years. This event was bigger than life to me and it started with the annual freshman orientation for new high school students.

This event was like no other, but before I share with you what it was like, I have to give you the backdrop. All of the students from the two middle schools in the city were scheduled to be there. I had the honor of attending East Middle School, home of the Vikings. I created so many memories there and I developed some strong friendships that would carry over to high school for the next four years. At East Middle School, we donned the red and white and wore those colors with pride. I wore my Vikings gear, as did most of my friends that lived on the Southside.

The Southside was something special in itself. Though there were many challenges associated with being raised in this area, there were also huge benefits, namely the family-like atmosphere in the neighborhood. To live on the Southside was a source of pride for all of us as we prepared to enter the high school ranks.

Our archrival was West Middle School, home of the Mustangs. They wore blue and white. A lot of kids who lived just a few blocks down from me or who lived in the west section of town went there. This would be the first time, outside of the various sporting events and parties we often attended, all of the students would come under one roof as the new freshman class. We were no longer rivals, we had become one body known as the Braves. I could barely wait to get there and develop these new relationships.

In preparation for the orientation and school year my mother took me shopping to get new school clothes. Some parents have a bad habit of spoiling their children for these types of events. I was lucky because my mother would scrape up what she could in order for me to look nice, even if I didn't deserve it. If you are in a similar position now, you ought to be grateful because there are many kids who don't have the privilege of sporting the latest fashions to show off their swag. They simply can't afford it.

We had a shop downtown everyone would visit to get the latest and greatest school clothes. They had an annual event called the Midnight Madness Sale. You were sure to find some killer deals. As far as style, the early 2000's were filled with jean jacket "hookups", forty nine 50's (baseball caps), colored wave caps, and throwback jerseys. My closet was full of them.

I was swaged out for orientation in my favorite outfit and I was ready for the world. Not only would my school pictures show me in a fresh new look, I was slated to get a new student ID, a locker assignment with the combination code for the lock, and my class schedule. The greatest thing I had been anticipating all summer long was the opportunity to meet all the new young women from West. This was going to be the highlight of my orientation experience. There was no greater sight for a teenage boy. Talk about excited!

What I didn't understand was the way you start does count for something, especially in this journey of high school life. My priorities were all out of whack. I had set my heart on things that really didn't matter.

What I should have been doing was focusing on how to get to my future classes instead of where all the popular kids were hanging out. Instead of worrying about what I would wear to impress the masses, I should have been concentrating on how I would wear my thinking cap in lectures. As you prepare for high school or if you are currently in the thick of your journey, know this one thing: dominating high school and becoming successful starts in 9th grade.

The first day of class was my time to shine. I had already made friends on the freshman football team due to our early summer practice schedule. I also knew some of the kids from the other middle school because I had competed against them in basketball and track. My older sister attended my high school so I knew a lot of her friends as well. In my mind, these connections set me up for immediate popularity. I was on the fast track to stardom. Unfortunately I had yet to consider the importance of starting strong academically. All I could think of was socializing.

I wasn't a bad student. In fact, I was a 4.0 student all throughout middle school. None of that mattered now. None of your previous accomplishments means much now that you have entered this new arena. How can I say that? It's experience. It's because the challenges you will face are tougher than before. The distractions are louder than before. The success is more gratifying and the failure cuts deeper than ever before in high school.

In the same light, none of your previous setbacks matter much. This can be a fresh start. You can come into high school with the decision already made in your heart that you are going to give it everything you have. This is why I am writing this book. I wish someone had taken the time to really prepare me for what was coming. I wish someone had told me the importance of fighting like a mad-man, academically, to see my success come to fruition. At this level of the game, it's either sink or swim. You must run through walls designed to keep you trapped in mediocrity. Better yet, pick up the key lying before you called "effort". This key unlocks the door to your destiny.

So how did we start? Well, we had been sleepwalking through much of the first semester. I'm not saying we failed all of our classes and we were terrible students. No, that is not the case at all. What I am saying is we didn't reach our potential. Many of us took for granted our academic history. I thought I could breeze through the freshman level courses and I didn't apply the same vigor in the classroom as I did in my other passions. Many of us fall into this trap. We come to class every day focused on the non-essential facets of the high school culture, but never tap into the wealth of learning. Don't get caught in the trap.

In order to dominate your high school journey, you have to start strong. You may be asking yourself, "How do I do this?" It starts with the right mindset. You have to know what you are in high school for. It's not so you can meet that new boyfriend and girlfriend. It's not so you can have a great time playing sports. It's not because your parents are making you go. It's not any of those things. The primary reason for your attendance in high school is to get an education so you will be equipped to excel in the next phase of your life. Without education, society declares you are primed for failure. You have to adjust the way you think as it pertains to your academics. You have to get pumped up and excited to academically dominate high school.

One mistake I made was sitting in the back of class. Nothing good happens in the back. That same drive and determination you show when you want to be the first in line at practice, should be displayed with your academics. Sit in the front of your class. Change the assumptions your teachers and the faculty may have about you. Let them know up front that you are here for business. Come ready to learn and engage. If I could use a sports analogy or coach's speech to bring further clarity on dominating high school, it would be something like this:

- "Your objective is to totally dominate your opponent! This means that you go as hard as possible on every play, on every down, in every quarter, and in every game. You do this until there is nothing left for you to give. When you look up and see **0:00** on the clock you can shout that you are victorious! That you have defeated the obstacles that lay before you. That you have conquered high school!"

This is the type of declaration you have to encourage yourself with. To declare is to make known or state clearly. It means you are announcing something. You have to become a positive thinker as it pertains to your ability to dominate your classes. You have to start strong and equip your mind. You have to make a public service announcement to yourself that you won't be held back by ignorance any longer, and you are going to dominate your challenges. If I could have done things differently, I would have started my high school journey with this type of mentality. I would have given that same motivational speech to myself every single day.

If I could turn back the hands of time, I would have gotten off the bus each morning with business in mind, not focusing on who I would cap (joke) on that day. I would have stopped wasting my time freestyle rapping with my friends in the hallways when the bell sounded and class had begun. I would have focused more on math formulas and the periodic table, rather than which girls were a "dime piece" (a girl ranked the highest in beauty on a scale of 1-10) and who wanted to "kick it" (be in a non-committed relationship) with me.

I wouldn't have tried to be the center of attention and lobbied for votes to become Homecoming King. I wouldn't have come home every day and turned on the television, or taken a nap and neglected my homework until I got to my homeroom class, rushing to finish the next morning. If I had realized that my road to success started in 9th grade, things would have been drastically different. I would not have focused so much on the social aspect of my high school experience. I would have placed it in the proper position. Sports and recreation are important, but they are not everything.

If you start strong, declare your desire for success and stick to that positive mindset, your high school journey can be conquered. If you adhere to these principles, I believe you are destined to dominate!

CHAPTER REVIEW

1. Your journey of dominating high school begins in the 9th grade.
2. Despite our desire to socialize and experience the thrills of high school life, we must remain focused on the reason we are there. That reason is to gain an education that will set us up for future success.
3. Dominating high school starts with a mindset. We must encourage and motivate ourselves with a motivated declaration statement.

TAKE ACTION

Now that you understand your journey starts the very first day of high school, write a declaration statement, which is simply an announcement of what you intend to do. You can write it down on a piece of paper or in a journal. The declaration will speak to your desire to conquer high school academically. The more you speak your declaration, the more you will believe. Once you believe it, you can achieve it.

SAMPLE DECLARATION STATEMENT

"I believe that I will dominate high school academically. I am focused on achieving greatness. I will not allow anything to hinder my progress. This is my declaration."

Signed X Motivated Student

SOCIAL MEDIA CHALLENGE

Tweet "My journey of dominating high school starts now!" **@BattleLeaderGrp** and follow that up with **#D2Dbook**. This will let your followers/friends know you have begun your walk of domination.

"We all have dreams. But in order to make dreams come into reality, it takes an awful lot of determination, dedication, self-discipline, and effort."

- Jesse Owens

CHAPTER 2
KEEP THE PACE

Now that the race has begun and you've started strong off the sprinting blocks with a new declaration, you have to keep the pace. What does that mean? Well, you have to stay consistent and not waiver on what you said you were going to do. From the previous chapter's action item, you should have developed a well-crafted statement regarding your desire to dominate high school academically. You have to stay true to this declaration.

Keeping the pace doesn't mean you are over extending yourself or slowing down on your goal, but rather you are staying true to the process. It is acknowledging your challenges and your setbacks. It is identifying areas of weakness and places for improvement. It is celebrating your milestones, but not relaxing or abandoning the overall mission of dominating high school.

It is important that you make markers for yourself. These are checkpoints throughout your journey of high school. You may decide to place a marker after your first test in a class. Maybe you have a marker set after you have completed your mid-term assessments. You could have a checkpoint during Thanksgiving or Christmas break. Whatever the time you decide to mark down go all in from start to finish.

This type of system will help you keep up the intensity. It is easier to exude maximum effort when you know it will end at some point. When you reach a marker or milestone, you can exhale. You can take a rest. This doesn't mean you lose focus, but it means that you have time to reflect on the portion of the race you just completed.

When I played football in high school, there were conditioning drills we had to perform successfully before we could put on the pads and begin cracking heads (i.e. full contact drills). As a part of our conditioning program, we had a test called "THE EDGE". In this conditioning drill, half of the team would line up at the top left hand corner of the football field and the other half of the team would be positioned at the opposite right hand corner.

Our coach would blow his whistle for the first person in line to sprint diagonally across to the other side of the football field. He would blow his whistle each passing second and signal for the next person in line to begin sprinting. The key to this exercise is to run as hard as you could to the other end. Once you reached the corner of the end zone, you would turn and jog up the corresponding sideline.

At first glance, it seemed intimidating and unbearable to participate in such a challenge, but THE EDGE wasn't as bad as I thought it would be. I learned to conquer it. When sprinting down the field, you give everything you have. Every bit of energy, every ounce of determination, and every fiber of your being is given toward the sprinting portion of this test.

When I came to the sideline jog, I worked on my breathing in order to recoup from all of the energy expended during the sprint. I would lightly gallop down the sideline and mentally prepare for the next round. I rehearsed my declaration statements or the goals I set for myself and would proclaim things like:

- "Nothing can stop me from dominating this race!"
- "I am the leader on this team and I have to be an example."
- "This conditioning can't beat me, but I'm going to destroy it!"
- "If I just push myself a little harder and go a little longer I will set myself apart from other players."

These sayings would go through my head during my time of rest on the sideline. It was motivation and fuel to my fire for the next round. I set a goal of playing varsity football as an underclassman, which I accomplished. I set a goal of becoming an all-conference player, which I achieved. I was determined to get the opportunity to play at the collegiate level and it became a reality. You have to set goals for success in your life. While you are in your time of rest, begin reflecting on the goals you have made and see yourself accomplishing them.

How does this compare to the goal of graduating from high school? It relates in a great way. When you're taking that math class and studying the various concepts, you give it everything you have. You make sure you go to study table. You meet with tutors. You ask questions and participate in the discussions of your class. You do not leave anything to chance, you conquer mountains throughout your high school journey.

When you get to your pre-designed marker, you work on your breathing. This means you take a deep breath and reflect on the things you did right and the things you may have slipped up on. Now you take that experience and prepare for the next portion of the test. This is how you keep the pace. You give a great effort. You take a break and reflect on the process, preparing yourself mentally to get back at it. Just like my football team did when we ran THE EDGE, you must do the same thing when running the race of your high school life. If you keep the pace by giving maximum effort during the sprinting portion of your race and reflect on your goals at each marker, I believe you're destined to dominate!

CHAPTER REVIEW

1. A key to dominating high school is keeping the pace.
2. Just as our football team did, you must run the sprint portion of THE EDGE as hard you can. This means you go full speed at studying, receiving tutoring, and participating in classroom discussions.
3. Use your rest time to reflect on the things you did well and the areas you need work. Once you have recouped mentally, get back in the game.

TAKE ACTION

Assign checkpoints or markers to your high school journey. These could be key points in your semester like quizzes and mid-terms. They could also be times that you have vacations like Thanksgiving, Christmas, and spring break. Reflect on your effort during these times and rehearse your declaration statement. You will get stronger with each marker you successfully complete.

SAMPLE OF THE EDGE

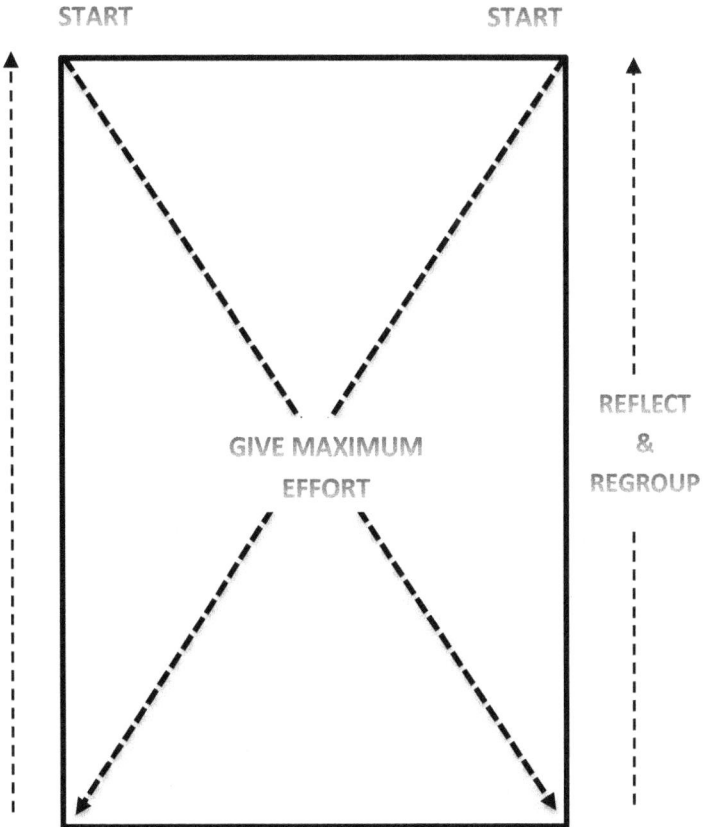

START   START

GIVE MAXIMUM
EFFORT

REFLECT
&
REGROUP

SAMPLE MARKER/CHECKPOINT LIST

Marker #1 - After Mid-Terms

Marker #2- After Thanksgiving Break

Marker #3 - After Final Exam

*Remember to take a rest between each marker. During this time, you want to reflect on the things you have done right and the things that challenged you. After your reflection, get back to it with maximum effort.

SOCIAL MEDIA CHALLENGE

Tweet "I'm keeping the pace of dominating my high school journey!" **@BattleLeaderGrp** and follow it with **#D2Dbook**. This will let your followers/friends know there's a consistent pace needed in order to dominate.

"Talent wins games, but teamwork and intelligence wins championships."

- Michael Jordan

CHAPTER 3
EVALUATE YOUR TEAM

Sometimes you have to do some things in your life that really seem to hurt. Get used to it. It is a part of your individual growth. Evaluating your team is one thing that causes pain. What I mean by this is determining who in your circle of friends is really for you and cares about your future. It also means identifying those individuals around you who do not have your best interest in mind. This step is crucial to your success of dominating high school.

We all have friends we have grown up with since the time of playing curb ball and running into the house before the streetlights came on. These friends know everything there is to know about you and your family. They know the good, the bad, and the ugly. They know the ins and outs of the neighborhood you grew up in. They have seen you in your worst moments and have witnessed you at your best. The problem is that sometimes these same people want to keep you in your worst and never want to see you operate at your maximum ability. This is why you have to evaluate your team. You do this by being honest with yourself and being honest with others.

You know when someone is trying to hold you back. They treat you differently. Never be intimidated by those who make the wrong choices when you make the right ones. Don't let low self-esteem kick in because you want to succeed academically and others are trying to make you feel bad about it because they don't agree with your choice. You have the right to dominate high school!

Many students have had experiences with their peers that left them feeling like dirt. Your friends may say things in passing that appear to be friendly jokes. These comments often have to do with your desire to excel academically. You may laugh those jokes off in an attempt to remain safe from ridicule, but please believe me, these types of jokes are meant to discourage you. Your friends' comments are a shabby attempt to keep you behind. It is a scheme to make you think intelligence is "un-cool" and it is a tactic to hold you back by others who have not made the decision to better themselves. When you consider these things, there is nothing wrong with evaluating your team. Just know that if you do not evaluate those who you hang out with, you may regret it forever.

After you have been real with yourself, you can begin the more challenging aspect of the evaluation process. This stage of evaluation is to have a real conversation with your so-called friends. If they can't support your decision to dominate high school life, then they can't roll with you. If you allow them to stay in their current position of influence in your life, it will handicap your ability to dominate. "You mean I have to actually have a conversation with my friends? The same person who respects my swag and has been around me pretty much my whole life?" Yes. I am saying you must develop the courage to stand up to those who secretly despise you. No friendship is worth working minimum wage at a fast food restaurant for the rest of your life because you refused to evaluate your team. That is the reality of the situation. Evaluation is necessary for growth.

You may have to separate from friends who appear to be going down the wrong path in life even if they are your BFF or your homeboy. Do your friends smoke weed, drink alcohol, or even get into more hardcore drugs like meth and molly? If so, you're playing with fire. It may be hard to believe but current statistics show that marijuana use among 8th graders has increased[1]. You've seen it in your own schools. Your friends may have gotten their first hit in junior high. Back then, and even now, getting high might have seemed like the cool thing to do. It may be appealing for the thrill but it's not worth forfeiting your destiny.

I don't want to sound like a *D.A.R.E.* (Drug Abuse Resistance Education) commercial but drugs are just stupid. Celebrities have made it popular especially in the music and entertainment industry, but its harm supersedes the potential good. Drugs have destroyed families. Mothers and fathers addicted to crack, have children left hungry at night because their last few dollars were spent on a fix. You may be one of those children who have seen drug use first hand. Maybe due to the impact of drugs in your house you have to scrap for food by eating a dollar pack of noodles or sugar toast for dinner. Drugs not only affect the person using them, they affect and destroy entire families.

As we will discuss later in this book, don't repeat the cycle. Don't let the financial burdens of your family or the desire for material things push you into selling drugs. That is a limited mindset. The entrepreneurial skills demonstrated by drug dealers are also used in the traditional work force or start-up project, but you have to realize it. To make it plain, say no to drugs regardless if you're doing them or selling them. For those students who hang out with drug addicts or drug dealers, the age-old adage "birds of a feather flock together" still applies to you.

Do you want to be labeled the same as those participating in illegal activity? Weigh the pros and cons. If you get caught smoking weed, doing drugs, or even being around these sorts of things, what will admissions counselors of colleges and universities think of you?

What type of job do you hope to obtain when they require random drug screening? Do you think it's possible to "outsmart" the process? If so, it will only happen for so long. The law of averages will eventually take place and the things you have gotten away with will catch up with you. Don't throw away your future with stupidity.

Evaluating your team also means that you take a serious look into your dating relationships. Now this is going to be difficult for many because you have invested so much into your boyfriend or girlfriend (also known as your Bae) and you don't want to throw it all away. For those of you who may be in a relationship right now, you have to ask yourself is the person you are dating helping you reach your destiny or are they keeping you locked in an emotional jail cell?

Does your boyfriend or girlfriend keep you captive when they don't respond to your snap chat (social media platform)? Do they keep you on edge when they ignore your direct Twitter message? How do they make you feel when they don't answer a good old-fashioned phone call? Are you spending entirely too much time with your girlfriend or boyfriend and not nearly enough time on your academics or with your family?

Do you feel obligated to spend your money on your boyfriend or girlfriend to keep them happy? Do they pressure you into areas of sexual activity you would rather not go? Are they helping you or hurting you? You have to evaluate if sticking out a high school relationship is worth your destiny. If it's not worth it, you may have to do the thing you fear the most and let that person go. If you do not develop the courage to address the situation, your boyfriend or girlfriend may be the trap that snares you on your high school journey.

When you review who is on your team, you may find some good things you didn't expect. In fact, you may find other individuals who want to commit to breaking the mold and dominate their high school life academically, too. There is always a remnant of kids who stand out, despite persecution from other high school students.

Some believe they will feel the wrath of those who just don't care about anything if they are labeled as being serious about their education. If anyone attempts to make fun of you for having the desire to better yourself, just let them know you are destined to dominate not only high school, but also your future. Mention to these individuals that if they desire to get out of the hood, get out of poverty and provide a better

21

life for their family, and make their parents proud, they should join you on the road to success and become a part of your domination team..

After you have completed your evaluation and you have identified those who are for you and those who are against your purpose, you need to make the split. There are no hard feelings in this matter. You may still have some friends you keep on your roster, but you can't hang out as you used to. You have newfound priorities. This is not meant to be a lifetime separation, but rather a time of focus and dedication to your educational journey. You must realize, at the end of the day, you will make of your future what you will. If you evaluate your team and remove those who are detrimental to your purpose, I believe you are destined to dominate.

CHAPTER REVIEW

1. Evaluating your team is necessary if you are going to move forward successfully in your high school journey.
2. Evaluation is necessary for growth. Not only to review your friendships, but it should also be done with your dating relationships (i.e. boyfriend or girlfriend).
3. Sometimes you have to do the thing that hurts the most in order to grow. This may mean ending a relationship adverse to your destiny.

TAKE ACTION

Take some time to evaluate who is on your team. You may want to write it out on a sheet of paper with two columns. On the left side column, list every person on your team who is supportive of your decision to dominate high school academically. These individuals should be willing to help you reach your destiny in any way.

On the right side column, list the individuals who do not have your best interest in mind. Once you have identified both groups begin having real conversations with these people. Help them to understand your purpose and what goals you have set to accomplish. You will see a noticeable change in your life while you continue dominating your high school journey.

SAMPLE TEAM EVALUATION CHART

TEAM EVALUATION LIST	
FOR YOU	**AGAINST YOU**

DOMINATION TEAM FINAL CUT
*(list your new team below)

SOCIAL MEDIA CHALLENGE

Tweet "I'm setting up my domination team!" **@BattleLeaderGrp** and follow it with **#D2Dbook**. This will let your followers/friends know that you are evaluating your team for success.

"Attitude is a little thing that makes a big difference."

- Winston Churchill

CHAPTER 4
ATTITUDE ADJUSTMENT

As a kid, I was very competitive in sports. Sometimes that competitive nature would get the best of me. To make it plain and simple, I had a bad attitude. I let my passion for the game fuel my selfishness. I could be downright nasty sometimes and it took many instances of correction for me to get the picture of my behavior. In order to be successful and dominate high school, some of us need attitude adjustments.

I remember one particular moment when I was a kid playing in a junior league basketball game. I was the only one scoring and there was no defense in sight from my teammates. We would go on to lose the game we were playing in. Throughout the contest, my attitude was horrible. I disrespected my coach on more than one occasion and I thought I was bigger than the team. I couldn't understand why no one else cared like I did.

Now that I am older, I can reflect on my past. It wasn't that any of the other players didn't care, but perhaps they simply couldn't perform the tasks asked of them athletically. Maybe I was just being a jerk. Perhaps there was more involved than winning and losing, like learning how to be a willing participant of a team and sportsmanship. These are lessons I had to learn.

It doesn't stop on the basketball court or the football field, it continues in the classroom and in the boardroom of corporate America. Your attitude goes a long way in contributing to your success or failure. If I was going to dominate high school, I needed an attitude adjustment.

Sometimes you just need someone to point out the obvious. I was immature. I cried and screamed at anything that didn't go my way. That type of behavior is not how a future business professional conducts himself or herself. That is not the way to be a productive member of society. Maybe you need to learn how to stop running your mouth and start opening up your ears and listening. This is the first step in your attitude adjustment. You have to listen to the guidance coming your way about your behavior. It is the main way to start the process of transformation.

Our generation also has a big problem with being disrespectful. During my time in high school, I witnessed teachers get cussed out by students. These educators would take the punishment from young people who didn't know better for several reasons. Maybe it's the influence from home where disrespect occurs regularly. Perhaps you are a student who wants to be a class clown for popularity. Whatever the reason, if this is you, stop it. End your negative behavior toward faculty and staff. Follow the golden rule: Treat others like you want to be treated!

This rule should be followed in high school hallways across America and throughout the world. End the torture perhaps you and others have inflicted on your peers. Bullying has gone too far. The U.S. Department of Health & Human Services defines bullying as the following:

- Unwanted, aggressive behavior among school aged children that involves a real or perceived power imbalance. The behavior is repeated, or has the potential to be repeated, over time. Both kids who are bullied and who bully others may have serious, lasting problems[2].

Maybe you don't agree with someone's lifestyle. Maybe you are a follower and not a leader. Perhaps you pick on other students because the crowd does it and you're scared to stand up for what is right. Whatever your reason for bullying, make a decision to end your efforts today.

You do not have the right to make life difficult for someone else when high school is already hard enough. It's happening in the inner city as well as in the suburbs. The driving force is always popularity and commercialism. Don't be a willing participant in this broken race for acceptance.

I believe if we can get a generation to pay attention, filter their words and check their attitudes; then maybe we will see a decline in suicides among teens. The Center for Disease Control and Prevention (CDC) states that youth suicide results in approximately 4,600 lives lost each year[3]. Again, it's not about your personal belief in one's lifestyle, rather it's about respecting humankind. The way you treat people can go a long way. If you ignore what I am sharing and you don't change your attitude, you are sure to end up on the wrong end of your destiny.

An attitude problem isn't only disrespect, it also has elements of low self-esteem and depression. Speaking purely from a place of experience of not believing in myself, low self-esteem and depression is real. When society's youth are dealing with depression and low self-esteem, it pushes them to the edge, with many desiring to jump off. They begin to fall into a downward spiral of pain, if not properly addressed. Drugs and alcohol become an escape that only leads to further destruction. The pain inflicted through cutting may seem like a temporary fix, but it leads to permanent scars, both inside and out.

I understand some cases may be more extreme than others and certain forms of low self-esteem, depression, and abuse, require some form of medical attention. However, students often just need a little encouragement. Sometimes a student needs someone to speak into his or her life with a positive affirmation. I want to encourage each reader to start thinking better of his or her self.

Don't let society determine your level of happiness. Don't allow the portrayals on television and on social media to influence your belief in yourself. Just as you made the declaration statement in chapter one, you can dominate high school. Begin to think of areas you are good or excel in. Don't focus on the negatives, highlight the positives. When positive words come out of your mouth, you begin to believe it. Confidence starts to form in you. You begin to think differently about whom you are and what you can accomplish if you put forth the effort. Try reciting some of these statements aloud:

- I am beautiful
- I am smart
- I am amazing
- I have a purpose
- I have a destiny
- I can do anything I put my mind to
- I will not be limited by my past
- I will be successful in my future

When you believe in yourself, courage increases and it gives you the ability to face challenges that plague you. Your attitude can adjust. If you heed these words, shift your thoughts, and change your attitude, I believe you are destined to dominate!

CHAPTER REVIEW

1. Your attitude can have an impact on whether you succeed or fail in your quest to dominate high school.
2. Address disrespect. Stop disrespecting your elders. This includes your teachers, faculty, and staff.
3. No one has the right to bully another person, even if you do not agree with certain life choices. Treat your peers with respect.
4. If a generation would filter their words and change their attitudes, perhaps suicide among teens would decline.

TAKE ACTION

Decide today that you are going to get an attitude adjustment. Look in the mirror and declare that from this day forward you will think positive about yourself and treat others with respect. Promise to the best of your ability, that you will respect teachers, faculty, staff, and even your peers. To respect someone doesn't mean you agree with their choices, it means you treat them as you want to be treated. Making this personal change will reap great benefits.

SAMPLE LIST OF ADJUSTMENT AREAS

Teachers - I will stop disrpecting them during lessons

Coaches -I will listen even when it hurts

Peers - I will stop bullying others who are not like me

Parents - I will stop talking back and not doing what I am asked

Personal - I will adjust my attitude about myself (self-esteem)

SOCIAL MEDIA CHALLENGE

Tweet "I'm getting an attitude adjustment for my destiny!" **@BattleLeaderGrp** and follow it with **#D2Dbook**. This will let your followers/friends know that your commitment to excellence and respecting others is valuable.

"The best way to not feel hopeless is to get up and do something. Don't wait for good things to happen to you. If you go out and make some good things happen, you will fill the world with hope, you will fill yourself with hope."

- *Barack Obama*

CHAPTER 5
GET INVOLVED

There is more to extracurricular activities than playing sports. One of the things I regret most about my high school journey was my decision to leave the concert band. For some odd reason I felt like I couldn't do both band and football. Because I was an athlete, I felt I had to spend most of my time getting better in my craft as an athlete. I was foolish to limit myself in this way.

If there is nothing else you gain from reading this book, know that you should never put limits on what you can achieve. You can do anything you put your mind to. I remember being challenged to play a particular piece of music one day in band class. I played the euphonium and I loved working with this instrument. I played the piece and did fairly well. After class, my band director came up to me and told me I had a lot of talent. He said if I worked hard, he could see me playing in the highest band level the following year. I was involved in something bigger than I could have ever imagined, but for some reason it didn't fit my image. I had participated in competitions with the concert band and we were successful in every event we competed in, but because of my sensitivity to self-image and popularity, I began to think playing in the band was for "geeks".

I can remember being on the football field after one of our grueling practices and seeing the marching band preparing for rehearsal. Attempting to be funny, and in order to be lifted up by my football buddies, I mocked the marching band. I acted like a complete donkey. I embarrassed myself and didn't even know it. Unfortunately, because of bad advice, a lack of confidence in myself, and a desire to fit in my supposed culture, I quit the band the next year. It was one of the biggest mistakes of my life.

Don't make the same mistake I made. Get involved in your high school. Even if it's in something that goes against the trend for you, just do it! Don't allow your peers to determine what you could and should be good at doing. Find out for yourself.

Other areas I participated in, in regards to extra-curricular activities, were Business Professionals of America (BPA) and DECA Marketing Club. These two opportunities took me to places I never thought I could reach. Sometimes it takes a teacher to see something good in you that maybe you didn't see within yourself.

I had one of these amazing individuals in my life that saw past my issues and complexities. This teacher helped me learn business and marketing concepts and prepared me to compete in BPA and DECA's various competitions. From these extra-curricular activities, I was able to make friends with students I may have never associated with before and met people from other places (who were not athletes) once I was challenged to step outside of my comfort zone. These individuals were just as passionate about business as I was about football.

I was able to be part of a three-person small business management team that placed first at the regional, state, and even the national level for BPA. Our advisor was willing to reach into her personal pocket to help fund our trips to compete. When you operate in your purpose, people are willing to help see your vision happen. She did that and so much more. I honor her for the sacrifices she made to see us become successful.

Not in my wildest dreams did I believe we could win a national championship against teams that had more funding and resources than we did. We were from an economically-challenged inner city area. This was especially true in our school district. Our high school business club wasn't known for being very competitive.

Regardless of all the challenges, we still made it. From this opportunity, I had the potential to study business at a nearby university with a scholarship. Although I did not take this scholarship, I earned it. This is the result of hard work and getting involved. Take note of my story because it could be yours. Many of you could become the next regional champion in business marketing and sales. Perhaps some of you will be recognized for your musical gift by playing the violin or some other instrument. Getting involved is essential for your future success.

Another way to get involved is to become a creator. Often, college admissions groups like to see students be "self-starters" and organizers of different events. Volunteerism falls into this category. Have you ever volunteered for anything in your community? Are you aware of the troubles your community faces and in which ways have you decided to make a difference? These are valid questions that should be presented to a student looking to dominate their high school life and journey.

An example of a volunteer effort you can develop is a canned food drive. This is one of the more basic and budget neutral volunteer efforts you can make. You simply get permission from your local high school administration and collect as many cans as possible and donate them to a local food bank or non-profit organization that helps out families in need, especially during the winter months. You can even do something fun like organizing a thrift party. Instead of spending hundreds of dollars for your winter formal dance, get students to wear clothing from the local thrift store. These are fun ideas that will look good on your resume.

This is what it means to get involved. Don't just sit on the sideline, become a contributor to your high school. Have a voice others listen to and be a person people can look to for leadership. I believe if you heed these things and get involved that you are destined to dominate!

CHAPTER REVIEW

1. Extracurricular activities are more than just playing sports. This also includes getting involved in some of the after school clubs and organizations available.
2. Concert band and Orchestra are excellent extracurricular groups that could bring about scholarship opportunities.
3. Don't allow what people say or think sway your decision of whether or not you will participate in extracurricular activities. Decide for yourself. Be willing to step outside the box.
4. Become a creator. Develop volunteer opportunities that will look great on your resume.

TAKE ACTION

Getting involved in extracurricular activities is very important for your development as a student. When you participate in extracurricular activities, you are strengthening your leadership skills and broadening your horizons. Don't let other people dictate your willingness to engage your community and become a world changer. Try something new and volunteer your time. You won't regret it.

SAMPLE VOLUNTEER OPTIONS*

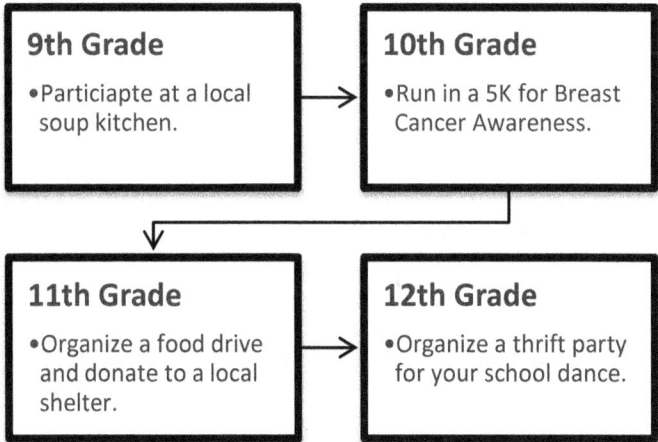

9th Grade

- Particiapte at a local soup kitchen.

10th Grade

- Run in a 5K for Breast Cancer Awareness.

11th Grade

- Organize a food drive and donate to a local shelter.

12th Grade

- Organize a thrift party for your school dance.

*These are suggestions of things you can do to get involved. You can decide in which order and what activity you want to do in your area.

SAMPLE EXTRA CURRICULAR ACTIVITIES[4]

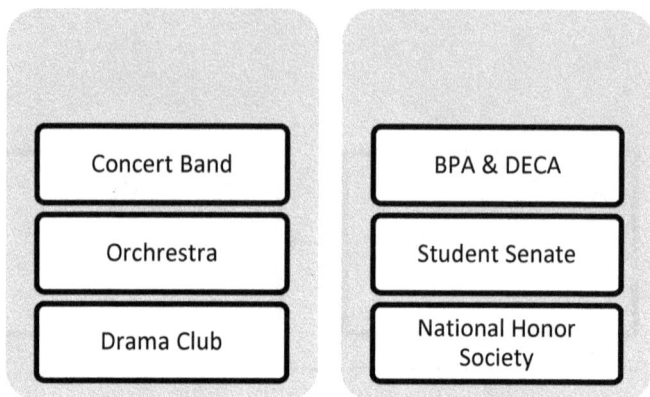

Concert Band	BPA & DECA
Orchrestra	Student Senate
Drama Club	National Honor Society

SOCIAL MEDIA CHALLENGE

Tweet to **@BattleLeaderGrp** and let us know you are getting involved in your high school or simply state "This year I'm getting involved in my school's extracurricular activities. I'm a creator!" Follow with **#D2Dbook**. This will let your followers/friends know your commitment to volunteerism and social awareness.

"I've got a theory that if you give 100% all of the time, somehow things will work out in the end."

- Larry Bird

CHAPTER 6
ATHLETIC SCHOLARSHIPS

My dream had always been to play college football. All of the practice time, all of the sports camps, all of the hours spent in the weight room, and all of the sweat and tears were to help me achieve an athletic scholarship. This is the dream for so many young people in high school. However, it takes more than athletic ability to earn a scholarship. It also takes hard work in the classroom. I think it is important to share my experience with this process to give a more realistic view of what it takes to be successful in this endeavor.

I wasn't the fastest athlete, nor was I the strongest kid on my football team, but what I did have was an understanding of the game and how it was to be played. I used this knowledge to my advantage. I was able to play varsity as a sophomore and I excelled my junior and senior years. I became one of the team captains and was able to gain valuable leadership experience. I can remember sitting in class my 11th grade year and having a letter delivered to me. It was from Columbia

University. My eyes lit up with excitement. My heart started to beat violently. I quickly opened the letter. It wasn't a scholarship offer. It was an inquiry of my interest in the Ivy League institution. I couldn't believe I was receiving a letter. Of course, as I grew older, I understood similar letters go out all the time to college prospects, but for me this was the silver lining in the sky I was looking for. That little letter helped to give me more drive and determination to achieve my goal. Sometimes a small victory is fuel to your dream. It will keep you moving in the right direction.

After the first taste of the recruitment process, I continued to work hard at my craft. I attended summer football camps at the University of Michigan and was able to see what big time college football looked like. I had the chance to meet many of the coaching staff from the early 2000s and was able to see how it felt to sleep and hang out in the dorms. I knew then I wanted to play college football.

I was fortunate to participate in this type of organized event. Many of my friends didn't have parents who were willing to shell out the fees associated with the football camps. For those of you who do have parents able to help you financially, do them a favor, appreciate them and be respectful of their sacrifice. It's not easy to pay $300 for a two or three day football camp when you're a single parent. If you do not have parents able to help you in this way, there are some alternatives. If you belong to a local place of worship or community group, try asking for a sponsorship. Perhaps your coaching staff may be able to assist you or even provide a free or low-cost alternative event. Do not feel like you can't accomplish your dream because of the roadblocks in front of you.

I want to encourage you that you can do it. Don't let anyone tell you that you can't make it based upon your family's economic status. Believe in yourself with everything you have.

Now, for the reality of the recruitment process. If your grades suck, you are not getting a scholarship! I am sorry to be so blunt, but let's be honest with ourselves. Many of the young people in high school right now believe they can achieve this feat without putting in the effort. It doesn't happen that way, and if it has for someone you know, that luck will catch up to him or her. You can't cheat life and the moral principles we all abide by. What you put in is what you get out.

Some of my teammates, friends, and even family members wondered how I was being recruited at the collegiate level. Sure, I was a decent athlete and I had impressive statistics for a 5'7 and 150-pound safety. I knew the secret to my success. I was excelling in my classes. After I shook loose from the start of my 9th grade year and began to focus, I was able to enroll in college prep classes. This got me noticed by several Ivy League schools and Division 1-AA (now known as *FCS* Level) schools that had stringent entrance requirements. This is the secret I want to share with you: If you are a better than average athlete who has a great work ethic, leadership ability, and a desire to be victorious in the classroom, there is an opportunity for you at the next level.

I attended Western Michigan University's summer football camp my senior year. This was a change from attending the University of Michigan's football camp because I knew I would have a better shot getting noticed by college recruiters if I switched venues.

I took everything I'd learned, all I had worked on and displayed my talents. I won the "Most Valuable Defensive Player Award" for my camp performance there and it gave me extra motivation to keep going.

Soon after the summer football camp at WMU, I began my final season in high school. I had finished my career on a good note and even though we didn't make the playoffs, which were a goal of mine, I did accomplish much through leadership. In this experience, I learned a great lesson on effort and sportsmanship. It's not always about wins and losses, but character building.

After the season, I continued to receive correspondence from several Ivy League programs, as well as Division 3 and Division 1-AA (FCS) teams. This is when I encountered Valparaiso University. I was noticed not only for my athletic ability, but also for my academics. Eventually, my classroom performance afforded me the opportunity to live my dream and play college football. Here is the main point I want you to get. No matter how gifted you are in basketball, baseball, football, track, or any other sport you participate in, the way you perform in the classroom is just as important as your athletic accomplishments. Your goal should not be to dominate the athletic field, it should be to dominate high school in every aspect and in every phase. If an athletic scholarship is really a dream of yours, make the decision today to put in the effort to obtain it. It can be done. As long as you put equal passion in academics and athletics, you can make it. I am a living testimony.

CHAPTER REVIEW

1. Young people don't realize that it takes more than athletic ability to earn a scholarship.
2. You must have as much passion in the classroom as you do on the athletic field or court.
3. Don't let your economic status make you feel like you can't make it in the athletic world. There are alternatives if you can't participate in the camp circuit.
4. There are opportunities to play at the collegiate level if you are an above-average athlete and display superior academic skills.

TAKE ACTION

Begin to adjust the way you think in regards to athletic scholarships. Just as you have developed goals to accomplish for your athletic season, become equally passionate about the goals you set for your academic season. Write them both out. If you become serious about both academics and athletics, there may be an opportunity for you at the next level. If you follow these principles, I believe you are destined to dominate!

SAMPLE ATHELETIC AND
ACADEMIC GOALS LIST

Freshman Year – I will make the honor roll, play AAU, and compete for a starting spot on the varsity basketball team.

Sophomore Year – I will continue to make honor roll, participate in sports camps and AAU, average a double-double, and start getting recruited by mid-major programs. Send film to schools and work on volunteering within the community.

Junior Year – I will continue to make honor roll and raise my GPA up to a 3.3, participate in sports camps and AAU, average a double-double, become a team captain and start getting recruited by power conference programs.

Senior Year – I will make the National Honor Society, raise my GPA to a 3.5, participate in sports camps and AAU, average a double-double, earn athletic and academic scholarships from a power conference program.

SOCIAL MEDIA CHALLENGE

Tweet "I'm going to dominate in recruiting." or "I will dominate my academics like an athlete does the field." **@BattleLeaderGrp** and follow it with **#D2Dbook.** This will let your followers/friends know that you have an equal amount of passion for sports and academic success.

"Education is the key to unlock the golden door of freedom."

- George Washington Carver

CHAPTER 7
ACADEMIC SCHOLARSHIPS

For many of the friends I grew up with, paying for college was a major concern. Most families just didn't have the finances to take care of their children's education. This is why athletic scholarships were important as I shared in the previous chapter. However, what is lost in the conversation of financial aid is the good old-fashioned academic scholarship.

Many youth only think of what their athletic ability will do for them and how it could help their families supplement educational expenses if they receive a full ride. I am here to encourage you to, not only fight for an athletic scholarship, but to open your eyes to the possibility of obtaining an academic scholarship. If you put your mind to it, you can obtain necessary funding to help you pay for college.

Will it take hard work? Absolutely, anything worth receiving will take great effort.

So how do you do it? Well, for starters, you can follow the tips I have shared throughout this book. Start by realizing your journey begins in the 9th grade. You can't afford to wait until you're in your junior or senior year to start getting serious about your academics. Start strong out of the gate by making it a priority to do well every semester you are in school. Tackle the giants in front of you. Once you come to the understanding that the world is not going to give you anything free, you can develop a determination that will push your dreams into arm's reach.

Start talking with your guidance counselors about what you need to obtain an academic scholarship. The misconception is that it's purely academic in nature. Albeit, most scholarship committees are looking for great merit rank, they are also looking for your involvement in extracurricular activities. What did you participate in while you were in high school? Were you a leader? Did you develop character traits only available through team settings? This is an important area both colleges and universities look at when evaluating their candidates.

Another area scholarships can be obtained is through admission into smaller, private institutions. Smaller colleges and universities are looking for individuals who stand out and are willing to become a successful student and contributor to their campus. The tuition rate sometimes scares families off from applying. Fear instilled by the "sticker-price" can be soothed by the realization of scholarship availability. Not only are private colleges a great place to look for academic scholarships, I also recommend looking into community colleges. Students can obtain full-ride scholarships if they have shown amazing academic history throughout high school. This may also be an option for families in tough financial situations. The view of community college is shifting in this harsh economic time. Many people used to consider community colleges "second-rate", but now these institutions are implementing strategies to better prepare students for the marketplace. They also have transfer friendly programs that can place you into many of the nation's most prestigious universities.

Regarding community and private colleges, plan to visit these campuses early; opportunities can spring from these visits. You may receive valuable information that otherwise would not have been shared if you hadn't visited the campus.

Selecting a major with limited representation is another way to find a scholarship. The world is always in need of teachers. Scholarships and grants are often available for students interested in this field based upon sheer need. Look into STEM fields (science, technology, engineering, and mathematics), which are sure to present some great scholarship opportunities as well.

You can also find scholarship opportunities by category. Minority students may have success by searching for scholarships specifically designed for them. Scholarships and resources are available based upon a ton of unique search criteria. You may find something tailor-made just for you.

Another thing to keep in mind is we are living in the age of technology and you should be using it, especially for researching scholarship opportunities. The internet is a harvest field for finding all kinds of scholarships. I suggest visiting federal websites that have incredible resources. One beneficial website in particular is www.studentaid.ed.gov. This site gives information on preparing for college, the different types of financial aid, how to apply for aid and, if you receive federal student loans, there is information on how to repay them once you graduate from college[5].

You may also find success with obtaining a scholarship on www.fastweb.com. This is one of the more reputable scholarship search engines in the higher education industry. Not only do they assist you with scholarship searches, they can help students with jobs and internship opportunities.

Your community is another place to look for scholarships. Many available resources are right around the corner from you. Places of worship and nonprofit organizations often have scholarship funds for their members. Checking with your local chamber of commerce and even investigating resources at your local library may be beneficial as well.

Lastly, speak to your guidance counselor regarding ACT and SAT prep courses. Do not wait too long to begin practicing for these mandatory entrance exams. The sooner you begin working on it, the better. If you are unable to pay the required fees for these tests, check with your guidance counselor and ask about assistance programs that help with funding. I would also encourage you to check with local organizations that may offer free practice testing. The more chances you have to take this test, the better you will score. A world of scholarships can open up to you if you do well on either the ACT or SAT, or both.

One of the most important aspects of the scholarship search process is developing an essay template for scholarship applications. During your search for scholarships, you will find a large majority of them require a corresponding essay. In this essay, one typically shares their background; they highlight their accomplishments and explain why they deserve the honor of the scholarship opportunity.

Due to the amount of scholarships you will apply for, it is a good thing to have a template prepared so you don't have to write a brand new document each time you apply for an opportunity. Having a template allows you to switch out necessary and key information. It will also allow you to keep the consistent parts that appear in most scholarship essays. Once your essay template is developed, you will want to save it to your computer or a flash drive you can take with you and have available whenever you get ready to complete a scholarship application.

If you are proactive about searching for academic scholarships and plan early to participate in university entrance testing (i.e. ACT and SAT), you will be well prepared both mentally and financially when it is time to go to college. If you are serious about obtaining an academic scholarship and you follow the tips I have given, I believe you are destined to dominate.

CHAPTER REVIEW

1. You have to be willing to fight just as hard for your academic scholarship as you do for your athletic one.
2. Start searching for scholarship resources via the internet and federal websites.
3. Check with your local community foundations for scholarship opportunities.
4. Start early with ACT and SAT prep. The sooner and more often you take the tests; the better your chances are of scoring well. This can open up doors for scholarships.
5. Develop an essay template that will help cut time on applying for scholarships.

TAKE ACTION

Decide today that you are going to get an academic scholarship. Take the necessary steps to obtain it. Set up studying habits. Research the federal student aid website and other community scholarship opportunities with your local chamber and non-profit organizations.

SAMPLE ACADEMIC SCHOLARSHIP SEARCH PLAN

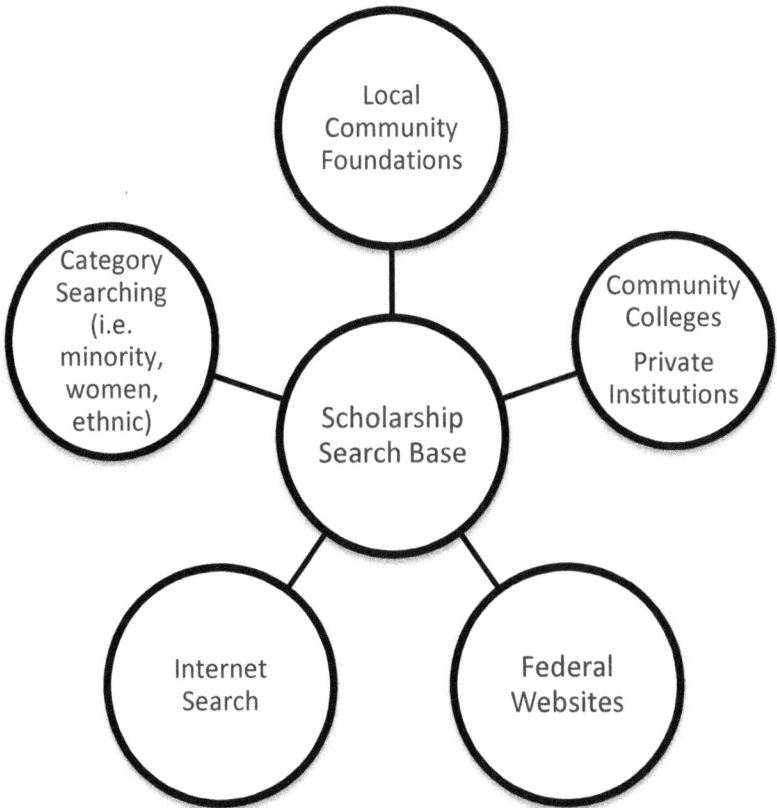

Local Community Foundations

Category Searching (i.e. minority, women, ethnic)

Community Colleges

Private Institutions

Scholarship Search Base

Internet Search

Federal Websites

SOCIAL MEDIA CHALLENGE

Tweet "I'm destined to get an academic scholarship!" **@BattleLeaderGrp** and follow it with **#D2Dbook**. This will let your followers/friends know you're determined to achieve academic excellence.

"The mediocre teacher tells. The good teacher explains. The superior teacher demonstrates. The great teacher inspires."

- William Arthur Ward

CHAPTER 8
REAL TALK SESSION (TEACHERS)

A good way to help a generation reach their destiny is to go right to the source. Teachers are the individuals who motivate, encourage, and equip our students every day. These educators are on the battlefield fighting for the lives of teenagers. Their experiences and perspectives are of great value. In order to help students dominate the high school life, I've gathered thoughts from those who work in the domain of education. In this chapter, you will find a collection of comments from educators currently serving in the field. One question I asked these individuals was, "What issues do you see happening with our students on a day-to-day basis and how can we help them?"

Here are some of their responses:

1. Family and generational failures

I think this is very critical. Some families are dealing with very complex issues. Often times these issues haven't come up overnight, but have been building for a while. Students have to deal with the challenges of high school as well as the challenges of home life. This may include assisting single parents with taking care of younger siblings (babysitting, feeding, washing, nurturing, etc.). It is difficult to remain mentally fresh in the classroom when you've been up all night because of chaos in the home.

Abuse is another area in the home that destroys the confidence of a young person. We see reports of sexual abuse more prevalently in the news. Many horror stories occur in that type of environment. If this is something going on in your life, I encourage you to speak with a guidance counselor or someone in the field you trust who can help you receive the healing you need.

Abuse is just not sexual, it is also verbal. There is no distinction when considering abuse; it all hurts. Perhaps you've been cursed out like a dog, and this has destroyed your self-esteem. Make up your mind, just as we communicated in the previous chapter, that you are going to think better of yourself. If no one has ever told you this, I am going to say it: You are an amazing person who has a great destiny before you. It's not about how you look, your popularity or any other material factor, it's about who you are on the inside. It is about how you treat people and respect yourself. It is about your work ethic and integrity. If you can accept this affirmation, you will be on your way to feeling better about who you are.

Family issues prevalent amongst our youth can also be generational. The problems that a student has are often the same ones their parents dealt with. The problems mom and dad went through twenty years ago, your grandmother and grandfather also experienced. This cycle continues to repeat itself generation after generation, but I would like to encourage you. No matter which mistakes your parents made, you are not subject to the same mistakes. You can overcome them. Even if relatives try to attach the same label to you, just believe in yourself. Declare in your heart that you are going to do something different with your life. Believe in your mind that you can be a world changer. Maybe your dad was never in your life. This is the case for many of our students in the urban community. Households are held hostage by the absence of the male voice. With no father around to affirm the identity of the child, confidence and a positive self-image disappears.

If this is something you are going through, don't be saddened. You can still become that man or woman you want to be. There are individuals you can look to for guidance and support. Maybe it's a coach, a mentor, a teacher, or a religious figure. It doesn't have to be one person. You can gain a ton of support from many different people, but you have to humble yourself to receive. The bottom line: don't let your family situation hinder your desire to dominate.

If you practice the principles in this book, you can overcome every obstacle. You can jump over every hurdle. You can bust through every barrier and dominate.

2. Addiction

This is a major issue with our young people today. Often we think our students are not doing drugs, but it does happen. We just don't know where to look. We look for the most visible drug, which is marijuana (weed), in our communities, and often miss many of the other more accessible drugs. A couple of drugs in particular are inhalants and prescriptions. Inhalants are chemical vapors people inhale on purpose to get "high." The vapors produce mind-altering and sometimes disastrous effects[6]. Something as simple as a marker could suffice for such a drug.

In regards to prescription drugs, they are some of the most accessible drugs to get high from on the market. These drugs are often unattended within the homes of naive parents. This is a disclaimer to lock up any prescribed medicine to ensure it is not broken into. As I stated earlier in this book, if you are doing drugs, stop it. Is it worth dying over? Is getting high worth spending the rest of your life behind bars? You definitely don't want to begin exploring the hard-core drugs of meth and cocaine. That level of drug use will surely take you down a road of darkness. Promise in your heart that you are not going to "turn up" by drinking and smoking, but that you are going to enjoy yourself in a safe way. Declare in your heart that you will surround yourself with positive influences. Make a decision in your mind that you will be the one to stand up and stand out against this type of activity.

Drugs are not the only thing this generation is addicted to; thousands of teenagers are addicted to pornography. Don't allow your curiosity to open

Pandora's Box. This type of unhealthy exploration can leave you in a place of ignorance, vulnerability, and with a distorted view of sexuality. I know it doesn't help to see risky images on television, on the internet and through social media, but you have the power to filter what you pay attention to. You can easily turn your eyes away from things that are detrimental to your success. Put restrictions on television. Delete friends who post negative and risqué images on social media. You can do it if you put your mind to it.

3. Teen Pregnancy and STDs

During my teacher interviews, not only was addiction a major issue, but teen pregnancy and STDs were a key concern. This is common among the youth of our nation and the world. Young people find themselves in tough situations as it pertains to sexual relations and teen pregnancy. Let's be honest, the greatest preventive measure for ensuring you do not get pregnant or obtain an STD is to keep your pants up! This is abstinence. You can ensure you are protected by setting limits on your relationship. Just don't go there.

Many in our generation are just plain lucky. Many kids didn't contract a virus or get pregnant not because they didn't participate in the act, but because they just missed the opportunity. Still, they played "Russian Roulette" by being oblivious of the facts and ignorant of reality. Don't become the statistic in your high school. Don't become the focus of the rumor mill. Don't become another color band on the wrist or a notch on the belt.

Our young men need to know it's okay to save

yourself for marriage and not lose your virginity to prove how cool you are. Don't let your peers pressure you into becoming sexually active just to fit in. Many of the young men in my community are looked upon as "punks" if they haven't done certain things. You do not become a man in this way. Manhood is defined by your work ethic, commitment to success, and respect for yourself and others. That is how you should define yourself, not by some jacked up standard composed by faulty men in your life.

Young women deserve better than to be stuck in the trap. You do not have to lie down with anyone to feel a sense of self-worth. This is no way to win the love of a person. Take a long look in the mirror and see yourself as beautiful. Not because of your outside appearance, but due to the inner strength, purity, and integrity you possess. Leave the parenting to adults. Don't become a kid with a kid. Don't allow your desire for intimacy, young women and young men, set you up for a sexually transmitted disease. It could cost you your life.

4. Anger

This generation has so much anger that, if measured, it could fill a stadium to its capacity. I, and others who work in higher education, have never seen so much built up animosity and angst. During these interviews, we found out a lot about a typical workweek in the life of an educator.

We see physical fights breaking out, students participating in self-mutilation, and verbal disrespect aimed towards themselves and others almost daily in many of our public schools. The assumption by most of society looking in from the outside is that the anger issue is due to a moral decline within our generation. What most don't seem to realize or acknowledge is that there is always a reason for a child being exceptionally angry.

One reason for the anger exemplified amongst our students is that something wrong or bad has happened to them. Their anger is a natural response to the wrong done to them. As I previously stated, issues at home are often a large factor for an angry young person. The lack of a father figure is a prime example. If this is the reason you have built up resentment and anger, I am not saying you shouldn't feel this way; anger is a human emotion. Acting on that anger is when you cross the line. Try talking it out with those you respect in a positive way, not hashing it over with friends looking to "geek" you up to do something stupid. The listening ear of an educator can provide a release of your anger in a healthy and therapeutic way, which can cause you to heal and grow instead of self-destruct. Middle and high school students are not the freak shows many depict them as being. They are teenagers full of passion and potential; they simply lack the knowledge that their purpose and destiny is immeasurably greater than the pain they have endured.

4. **Divorce**

Divorce is another area contributing to the struggles of youth across America. We are living in a world where commitment is foreign. Regardless of the situation, divorce has become more common and the collateral damage is often the children. Sometimes the divorce can split children with one parent or they have joint custody. This can often complicate the education process due to the strain of moving back and forth. Regardless of your adversity, I still believe you can rise above it.

Often, students feel responsible for their parents' divorce. If this is your situation, know that it isn't your fault and you couldn't prevent it. Instead of letting the divorce consume you, resolve in your heart that you will remain committed to your high school journey and finishing strong. Don't resort to drugs, alcohol abuse, cutting, and other activates to try to dull the pain you may feel. Let this also be a testimony to your resolve that, despite all you faced, you still were able to overcome it!

5. Popularity and Image

Another hot item identified through my teaching interviews was the desire to be popular. High school is an exciting time for students when they first enter as freshman. Some look for friends they can fit in with. Everyone wants to be accepted. The sooner one finds a group, the faster they settle into their role. Unfortunately, these roles do more harm than good.

A label can be beneficial in many ways. It helps you find things you need and identifies the contents of an item. The problem with labels in high school is they can be somewhat deceiving. First, the creator or designer of the product is not the one placing labels on people. In high school, it's your peers. Not everyone knows what is inside of you. People have a bad way of determining your story by looking at your outer appearance and attributes. Students can often miss the inner you! This is misrepresentation in high school. You can even mislabel yourself. Don't believe the hype. Trust your inner qualities and develop your strong suits. Label yourself as a person who respects others, works hard, and desires to dominate.

When students first start high school, they look to get involved in new activities and some even look for a new identity. Schedules are different and homework from every class can seem overwhelming at times. Ninth grade is such a culture shock to students and most do not realize it until it is too late. It is when their grades start to slip and they are running with the wrong crowd that they realize things should have been done differently. Popularity shouldn't be the apex of high school.

The desire for popularity is disturbing. One teacher shared a project her class conducted. She had each student write a letter to their eighth grade self. One student wrote that he would be excited because he was going to be the man in ninth grade. He did not plan to be lame like he was in middle school and would do everything he could to make sure he was popular, even going as far as getting in trouble often.

Students want so badly to be a part of the in-crowd that they do things completely out of character just to fit in. They change their hair, the way they dress, and say things to be down with a group who, tomorrow, they might not even get along with. It seems as though many students are stuck in an identity crisis that they are unprepared for because of the overwhelming culture of high school in general.

Even though ninth grade can be challenging, students should take time to discover who they are, what they like, and what they want to do in life despite what the in-crowd is doing. In about fifteen years, the in-crowd won't even exist and students will see those people at their ten-year class reunion and wonder why they wanted to be like them in the first place. Don't get caught in an identity crisis. Be comfortable in your own skin and desire to dominate the high school life and walk into your destiny.

During these interviews, each educator shared some unique insights about the challenges this generation faces. Many of these same challenges were present when I was in high school. There is so much pressure to fit in and identity is so important. If any of these testimonials touched you, try to take what they said to heart and do something about it. Don't follow the crowd. Don't allow anger to lead you down a path of destruction. Don't let drugs, alcohol, sex, and other addictions keep you from your destiny. If you follow the tips outlined in these teaching interviews, I believe you are destined to dominate.

CHAPTER REVIEW

1. You are not subject to the mistakes you have seen in your family. In addition, you can overcome the pain you may experience at home. You can still be successful.
2. Don't allow your desire for acceptance and longing for love to lead you down the road of drugs, alcohol, sexual activity and other addictions. It's not worth your destiny.
3. Anger is a normal emotion, but don't act on it. Find positive outlets that will help you through it.
4. Divorce is common now. If you have seen your parents go through a divorce, don't let it keep you from achieving your goals. You can still make it, despite the family setback.
5. Don't be consumed with fitting in with the crowd. Know that you are unique with gifts and talents. Find out who you are and be happy with that.

TAKE ACTION & REFLECTION

What can you do in response to the comments made by our educators? You may be unable to change your living situation at home or the challenges your family faces, but can you decide to remain positive and develop a strong support system? What about addiction? Are you willing to stand up against the use of illegal drugs and end relationships that promote negative behavior?

What about remaining sexually pure and putting measures in place to avoid sexually transmitted diseases?

Is anger a stronghold in your life? Do you seem to be consistently upset about something? Does respect or street cred weigh heavily on your heart? What can you do differently when faced with a potential blow up because someone disrespected you?

Will you allow anger to keep you from seeing the vast opportunities in the world? What about popularity and image? Does the desire for acceptance overwhelm you to the point you are willing to do anything to be the man? Do social media stats affect your identity? Reflect on these things and determine how you will overcome these situations. If you choose to do things differently, I believe you are destined to dominate.

SOCIAL MEDIA CHALLENGE

Tweet "I will not allow setbacks in my life to keep me from reaching my goals!" **@BattleLeaderGrp** and follow it with **#D2Dbook**. This will let your followers/friends know that the insight shared from these teachers spoke to you and you are taking their advice to heart.

"Our greatest weakness lies in giving up. The most certain way to succeed is always to try just one more time."

- Thomas Edison

CHAPTER 9
REAL TALK SESSION (STUDENTS)

We are dealing with a unique generation. What makes this set of youth so different from many others in times past is the ways they can be influenced, both positively and negatively. One of the reasons for this is the mass flood of social media into our homes. Students can't go a day without their cell phones, without updating their statuses, and sharing their favorite photos. As a result, opinions of others are at a premium amongst those in the hallways of our schools.

Not only is this a major issue, but as a society we are quick to judge and we rarely give youth the opportunity to speak and share their challenges. Many students are suffering with issues of self-confidence and failing relationships and this is why I decided to gather a sample of interviews and share some of their deep insights. I know what it's like to be a teenager in high school, feeling misunderstood, perhaps even hiding the scars that have defined us. I believe, through these testimonials, we may be able to inspire and encourage others in similar situations.

Review of Student Testimonial #1

Our first student testimonial highlighted the success and struggle of teenage girls. Student #1 expressed that many young women try hard to be the best they can be, considering the difficult challenges before them. She felt young teenage girls are often labeled as "easy" or that they play hard to get in regards to relationships. The reality is that many teenage girls are just trying to do the right thing in life. Many are unfairly labeled by society due to the failed examples shown to us from the media.

Student #1 shared that many teenage girls have detailed goals and dreams and many of them go on to graduate from college. To her, these are real examples of women who teenage girls should look up to. They are women who have overcome some of the negative stigmas given by society and are respected by their peers. Many of these women go on to obtain great careers and make a lasting impact in the business world.

In the interview, the student also shared that there are still negative examples influencing teenage girls in our generation. Her experience was that many young girls don't care about graduating from high school, college, or obtaining a career. The student indicated that these type of young women end up on the streets. In her eyes, this is primarily due to their lack of self-confidence. The student goes on to state the following:

- "Young girls face some rough times in their lives, especially when dealing with young men."

Her experience was that many young men hurt young women by cheating on them and doing other things that cause pain. The student communicated that spending time together is significant in relationships and if this isn't valued, your boyfriend doesn't deserve you. She went on to state the following:

- "Young men who always make up excuses or who are unfaithful to you are worthless. Those are the young men we need to stay away from. Those types will destroy you or make you lose focus on your life goals. A true young man will honor, respect, and help you achieve your goals."

In my review of this portion of the interview, it is obvious that relationships are a huge factor in high school. It would be foolish to ignore the impact of teen dating and how it affects your ability to dominate. Don't allow your feelings and emotions to hinder your destiny, especially for a boyfriend or girlfriend.

Another area the interviewed student shared as a concern was parental relationships. Across the nation and throughout the world, youth are often unable to see their fathers due to broken or divorced homes. The student shared from personal experience. She states:

- "I suffer a lot due the lack of a father in my life. I am unable to see him when I'm going through things. I can call him, but it's not the same. I want to be able to crawl into his lap and tell him what I am going through. I need him to listen to me. I just want my daddy to hold his little girl again."

Many students are dealing with the same sense of abandonment. Regardless of what happened in the past to cause a split in the parental relationship, youth are trying to navigate the lonely waters of fatherlessness. If you have a similar experience, know there are many individuals available to help fill that void in your life. They will never totally replace the father you never knew or seldom see, but they can provide some much needed guidance and direction to help you become the young man or woman you are destined to be.

Another enlightening area of the interview was the depth of bullying many of our young people are facing. This particular student was very transparent when it came to sharing the social challenges she faced amongst her peers. In regards to this, she stated:

- "I am a teenage girl who has been bullied since the fourth grade and I am still getting bullied to this day."

As we shared previously, bullying must end within our schools. Unlike any other time in history, young people are facing this form of intimidation because of the way they look, their economic status, their heritage, their desire to excel academically, and several other key factors. Not only does this generation face bullying, they also struggle with depression. A glimpse from the student:

- "I have struggled with depression, worthiness, and lack of confidence. My mother always tells me to look in the mirror and say, 'You are a beautiful, intelligent, and incredible young woman who can change the world with your beauty and smile'."

I believe parents should also take this approach to affirm their children. If you do not have a parent that pours wisdom into your heart, look to this book for inspiration. I agree you can change the world with your beauty and smile. When I say beauty, I am referring to the inner-beauty of integrity and respect.

I speak of the smile as an outward expression of attitude. No matter which obstacles stand in your way, you can overcome them if you embrace the right mindset. You can be the best that you can be. The student took the affirming words from her mother and began to believe she was, in fact, a confident, beautiful, and brilliant young woman. The more you make similar declarations, just as the student began to see a change in her confidence; you, too, will see a change in your life.

No matter what others say, when you believe in yourself none of the words spoken will deter you from walking in your purpose and achieving your destiny. Love yourself and do not let anyone bring you down was the advice the student wanted to share with others experiencing adversity in their lives.

- *8th Grade Student transitioning into High School*

Review of Student Testimonial #2

The second student we interviewed highlighted issues with laziness, detrimental desires, and poverty. From his perspective, he saw this to be more prevalent amongst fellow minority students. He believed teenagers often struggle with these issues because of perception, and their concern for social approval, especially from their peers. The way in which young people view society has guided their ideals about life. He went on to say:

- "We worship celebrities and believe that their lifestyle is the way we should conduct or mirror our lives."

Ultimately, this student believed our generation suffers from the desire to be like certain individuals we see on television, the internet, and throughout social media. We see the money, clothes, and cars and think that is all there is to life.

The reason we are star struck and fall for this perception is due to the lack of identity in this generation. The student believed this to be the case because, as a generation, we don't really have something greater to believe in. He capped his interview off by saying:

- "For those of us who have found something greater in life and have received an identity, it is our job to share that with others. We have the responsibility to help others understand who they are and how they can have a better life even as a high school student."

-   *10th Grade Student currently in High School*

In this interview, I perceived that the student truly understood what it meant to dominate. He didn't want to settle for anything less than excellence and walking in his purpose. He believed there was hope for students and people in general who don't believe in themselves.

I hope these two interviews have been encouraging to everyone who has read them and to those endeavoring to become successful. If you listen to the message these young people are sharing and see past your struggle, your insecurities, and begin to implement the principles shared, I believe you are destined to dominate!

CHAPTER REVIEW

1. Society and the media often label your generation. You can still succeed despite their opinions.
2. Relationships appear to be important in high school, but not to the point of forfeiting your destiny.
3. This generation is dealing with fatherlessness, but there are many mentors that can help guide you through your journey.
4. As a generation, we should strive for something greater. Once we find our identity, we have a responsibility to share that with others, in hopes they will also find their identity and purpose.

TAKE ACTION & REFLECTION

What comments made by the students resonated with you or really made you think? As a young woman, do you feel like you are labeled because of the images that are portrayed through the media? If so, how can you change that perception? Young men, are you chasing after material things as if that's the only thing that matters? How will you positively respond in this quest to dominate your high school journey? Decide today that you will not let anything hold you back from achieving your goals.

SOCIAL MEDIA CHALLENGE

Tweet "I will change the perception of my generation!" **@BattleLeaderGrp** and follow it with **#D2Dbook**. This will let your followers/friends know that you are going to stand up and dominate your high school journey regardless of what society thinks about you.

"Plans are nothing; Planning is everything."

- Dwight D. Eisenhower

CHAPTER 10
THE GAMEPLAN

In this chapter, I will review the game plan for dominating your high school journey. It will be a brief list of action items to follow over the next four years. You can also apply many of the principles to everyday life. It is as follows:

Year 1 (Freshman) - In year one, you will start strong, place your markers, adjust your attitude, and begin reaching for excellence in all you do.

- **Start Strong** - Come into high school or your new situation understanding why you are there, which is to dominate, especially academically.
- **Change your mindset** - Don't put all of your energy and focus into popularity, athletics, and relationships, but become passionate about dominating high school academically.
- **Write a declaration** - Write a declaration that

will speak to your desire to conquer high school academically. Rehearse this statement daily, weekly, or monthly. Adjust when necessary.

- **Create athletic goals** - Write out your goals for your athletic career (fifty tackles or 16ppg, all-conference, etc.).
- **Create academic goals** - Determine your academic goals (3.0 GPA, A+ on every test, etc.)
- **Develop a mentor/mentee relationship** – Ask your teachers, tutors, or coaches if they are able to give you advice and direction on how to succeed. Often times, they have a ton of information that just needs to be tapped into. Coaches can begin communicating the necessary steps for athletic scholarship opportunities. Advisors can point you in the right direction for academic scholarships and admissions guidelines.
- **Place your markers** - Obtain a calendar and place markers or checkpoints at different times throughout year one. These are times for rest and reflection. Regroup and get back at it once these times have concluded.
- **Evaluate your team** - Determine who will be a part of your inner circle for year one. With respect and sensitivity break off relationships that are detrimental to your life. Be open to relationships that are actually beneficial.

- **Get involved** - Get active with an extracurricular activity (BPA, DECA, Band, Orchestra, Robotics, Choir, Drama, etc.).
- **Change attitude** - Develop a positive attitude toward yourself, your teachers, and peers. Commit to respecting your fellow human beings.
- **Plan to volunteer** - Check into serving at a local soup kitchen or some other form of volunteering during holiday seasons. Make sure these activities are fine with your parents or guardian.
- **Review academic scholarship resources** - Visit the federal student aid website and review its content for 9th grade students.
- **Enjoy the process** - Allow time for fun. Just be safe and make good decisions. At the end of year one, you should have accomplished many things. Mark down every area you were successful and the areas that were challenging. Remember those things in the following year and continue to work on them.

At the end of year one, you can contemplate the progress that you have made on your journey of dominating high school. Reflect on your accomplishments and prepare for the next phase of your domination, which is your sophomore year.

Year 2 (Sophomore) - In year two, you will build on the foundation of year one by keeping the pace of domination.

- **Start Strong** - Come into your second year of high school or your new situation with a renewed passion to succeed. Get passionate about dominating high school academically again.

- **Write a NEW declaration** - Write a fresh declaration for your second year. This will give you a new perspective and updated vision for the year.

- **Create NEW athletic goals** - Write out your updated goals for your athletic career. Begin charting your growth and development. Research colleges and universities and fill out their recruiting inquire pages. If possible, attend sports camps before the school year and ask for film on your previous season to hand out to coaching staffs. Set a goal to be selected for the all-conference team in your sport of choice.

- **Academic goals & prep -** Update your academic goals (honor roll, dean's list, etc.). Check with your guidance counselor regarding ACT/SAT test prep. Begin checking with admissions reps regarding college and university visits.

- **Continue with your mentor/mentee relationship** - Allow the mentors you have received to continue assisting you on your journey of success.

- **Place NEW markers** - Obtain a new calendar and place markers or checkpoints at different times throughout year two. Remember to rest during these periods and reflect on your progress.

- **Evaluate your team** - Determine who will be a part of your inner circle for year two. Many relationships are seasonal. Perhaps you are in a new place of focus that will require you to do some things differently. Always evaluate your team.

- **Stay involved** - Remain active in the extracurricular activities you have joined and become a leader within these organizations.

- **Keep attitude in check** - Make sure your attitude remains in check when dealing with authority figures and your peers.

- **Continue volunteering** - Continue to pursue volunteer opportunities within your school and community.

- **Enjoy the process** - Make sure you have made time to enjoy your high school life in year two. Remain focused, but enjoy the moments you have.

At the end of year two, you should have a list of accomplishments that have contributed to your domination of high school. Continue to mark down areas of success and challenge. Reflect on how you can get better and start meeting with the mentors in your life more regularly. If you follow these principles and tips for year two, you are destined to dominate.

Year 3 (Junior) - Continue with most of the "game plan" as you did during the first two years. In year three, you will shift your focus toward future planning and consistency.

- **Start Strong** - Come into your third year of high school or your new situation with even more passion to dominate.
- **Write a NEW declaration** - Write a fresh declaration for your third year.
- **Create NEW athletic goals** - Write out your updated goals for your athletic career. Begin charting your growth and development. Continue corresponding with recruiters. Provide updated film of the previous year's highlights. Set a goal for all-conference and all-area or city.
- **Academic goals & prep -** Update your academic goals (honor roll, dean's list, etc.) and, if possible, take the ACT or SAT. The sooner the better, as most students take this exam more than once.
- **Continue with your mentor/mentee relationship** - Tap into the wisdom of mentors for year three. Pay special attention to their advice on character development and decision making. Allow your mentor to continue assisting you on your journey of success.
- **Place NEW markers** - Obtain a new calendar and place markers or checkpoints at different times throughout year three.
- **Evaluate your team** - Determine who will be

a part of your inner circle for year three. In this transition year, you are close to reaching the climax of your journey. Don't slip now.

- **Stay involved** - Remain active in extracurricular activities you participate in. Set goals to win competitions in your field and develop your craft for the future.
- **Continue volunteering** - Check into serving opportunities and you may even try developing some type of volunteer event yourself.
- **Enjoy the process** - Enjoy year three as you inch closer to your goal of domination.

At the end of year three, you should have accomplished a lot more by your dedication and effort. Continue to mark down areas of success and challenge. Reflect on how you can get better in preparation for your final year of high school. If you follow these principles and tips for year three, you are destined to dominate.

Year 4 (Senior) - In this last year, you will focus on leadership and finishing strong by obtaining a scholarship.

- **Start Strong** - Come into your fourth year of high school or your new situation determined to finish strong.
- **Write a NEW declaration** - Write a fresh declaration for your fourth and last year.
- **Create NEW athletic goals** - Write out your updated goals for your athletic career. Focus even more on your leadership. Continue corresponding with recruiters.

Provide updated film of the previous year's highlights. Continue visiting potential colleges and universities and obtain a scholarship hopefully.

- **Academic goals & prep** - Complete the ACT or SAT and prepare to finish strong academically. Finalize college applications and review scholarship opportunities. Set a goal to obtain a specific number of scholarships and get accepted into five colleges.
- **Place NEW markers** - Obtain a new calendar and place markers or checkpoints at different times throughout year four.
- **Stay involved** - Remain active in the extracurricular activities you have joined.
- **Continue with your mentor/mentee relationship** - Allow your mentor to continue assisting on your journey of success and begin to help to mentor others.
- **Continue volunteering** - Even at the close of your journey, you can still volunteer by serving the next generation. Look into reading opportunities at elementary schools or your local community center.
- **Enjoy the process** - Enjoy year four and celebrate dominating your high school journey.

At the end of year four, you should have reached your goal of dominating high school. At the conclusion of your journey, it is my hope the principles shared brought about a greater level of success for you. It is my hope you obtained an academic or athletic scholarship.

It is also my hope you obtained a greater sense of purpose and self-esteem has developed within you. Now you must prepare for the next phase of your life. If you apply what you have learned during your journey in high school to your next challenge in life, I believe you are destined to dominate!

CHAPTER REVIEW

Follow the bulleted lists for each year. Make sure you not only take every aspect of the game plan seriously, but that you take time to enjoy the process. Commit to excellence. Don't give up on your dream and goal of dominating high school. Recite your declaration statement. Keep the pace. Adjust your attitude. Give back to the community. Give an equal amount of effort in athletics, academics, and extra-curricular activities. Search for mentors that will share valuable wisdom on how to succeed. Decide today that you will be a leader in your generation.

SOCIAL MEDIA CHALLENGE

Tweet "I have a game plan to dominate high school!" to **@BattleLeaderGrp** and follow it with **#D2Dbook**. This will let your followers/friends know that you have a legit plan to make it through your high school journey and achieve your goal of academic success.

VISUAL PROCESS OF DOMINATING HIGH SCHOOL

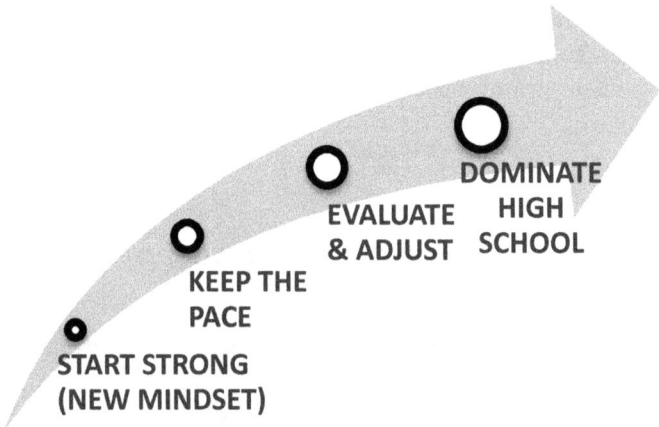

DOMINATE
HIGH
SCHOOL

EVALUATE
& ADJUST

KEEP THE
PACE

START STRONG
(NEW MINDSET)

BONUS INFORMATION
COLLEGE OUTLOOK

As you conclude your high school journey, particularly toward the end of your junior year, it is time to plan for your next phase, which includes some form of higher education hopefully. Take this time to think of several college options for public, private, military, and trade schools.

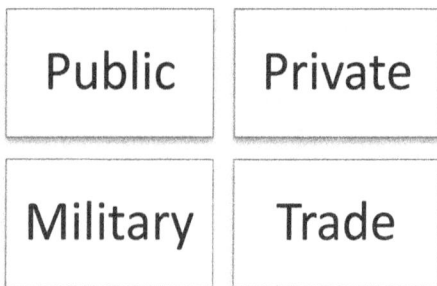

Public	Private
Military	Trade

Which schools come to mind? Is that school in state or out of state? Have you dreamed of applying to a private school? How about the Ivy League? Does the military interest you? Which branch? How about a trade school?

These are the types of questions to ask, as you are coming to the close of your high school journey. Start planning for college. See yourself thriving in whichever school you choose.

BONUS INFORMATION
FUTURE OUTLOOK

As you continue to dominate your life's challenges here are some additional things to consider. Where are you going? Have you begun to think about career options? How will you leave your stamp on this world? The following are different areas you may be destined to dominate:

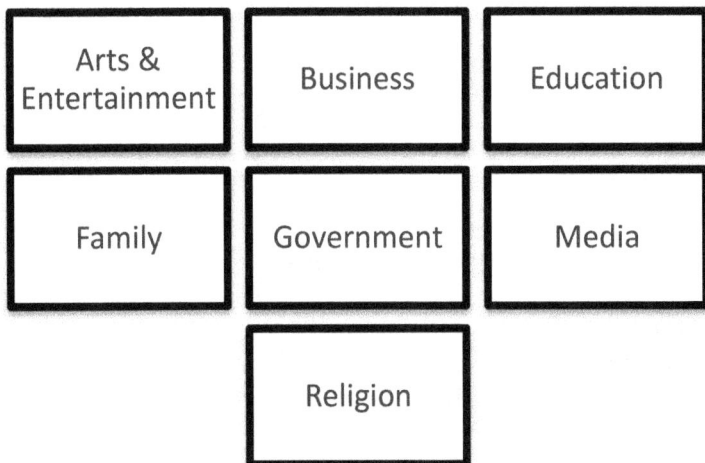

Arts & Entertainment	Business	Education
Family	Government	Media
	Religion	

Reflect on these domains and begin thinking about your role in one of them. Can you see yourself as a lawyer, doctor, artist, or teacher? Start planning now and you will become just what you dream of being.

CONTACT INFORMATION

P.O. Box 81189
Lansing, MI 48908

Email – info@battleleadershipgroup.com

Social Media:
www.facebook.com/battleleadershipgroup
www.twitter.com/BattleLeaderGrp

Twitter hash tags (#):
#d2dbook
#destined2dominate

Website:
www.battleleadershipgroup.com

ABOUT THE AUTHOR

Author, DeMarquis R. Battle is the founder and president of Battle Leadership Group LLC. He is an up and coming servant leader within his generation. He is a visionary, entrepreneur, higher education professional, mentor, and speaker.

He holds a Bachelor of Arts degree from Siena Heights University and two Master of Arts degrees from Grace College & Seminary and Lincoln Christian University. He has also completed postgraduate studies in Effective Leadership and Global Business Strategies from Davenport University. He is married to his beautiful wife, Raynika Battle, and they have two children, Justus and Olivia-Grace.

DeMarquis R. Battle is also the author of Don't Bow: Standing against the Idols of Our Generation. He continues to write, speak, and provide resources for the community, non-profit sector, systems of education, and the marketplace.

REFERENCES

[1] Drug facts- prescription drugs. (2014). Retrieved February 26, 2014, from http://teens.drugabuse.gov/drug-facts/marijuana

[2] Bullying definition. (2014). Retrieved February 26, 2014, from http://www.stopbullying.gov/what-is-bullying/definition/index.html

[3] Youth Suicide-Suicide Prevention-Violence Prevention-Injury Center-CDC. (2014). Retrieved March 6, 2014, from http://www.cdc.gov/violenceprevention/pub/youth_suicide.html

[4] For more information on Business Professionals of America and DECA Marketing club please visit http://www.bpa.org/ or http://www.deca.org/

[5] Studentaid.ed.gov. (2014). Retrieved March 5, 2014, from http://studentaid.ed.gov/

[6] Inhalants - NIDA for Teens. (2014). Retrieved March 6, 2014, from http://teens.drugabuse.gov/drug-facts/inhalants